20th Century Lives

ACTIVISTS

Philip Steele

PowerKiDS
press.

New York

Published in 2011 by The Rosen Publishing Group Inc.
29 East 21st Street, New York, NY 10010

Copyright © 2011 Wayland/
The Rosen Publishing Group, Inc.

First Edition

Designer: Jason Billin
Editor: Nicola Edwards

Library of Congress Cataloging-in-Publication Data

Steele, Philip, 1948-
Activists / by Philip Steele. — 1st ed.
p. cm. — (20th century lives)
Includes index.
ISBN 978-1-4488-3292-7 (library binding)
1. Reformers—Biography—Juvenile literature. 2. Social reformers—Biography—Juvenile
literature. 3. Biography—20th century—Juvenile literature. I. Title.
CT105.S827 2011
303.48'40922—dc22

2010024106

Photographs:
Getty Images: AFP; title page: Corbis: Bob Adelman, Camera Press: Gamma/Eyedea p. 12,
Simon Daniel/Gamma p. 22, Rob Welham p. 23, Keystone-France p2. 5; Corbis: Bob
Adelman p. 1, Bettmann p. 4, Bettmann p. 6, Bettmann p. 9, Interpress/Kipa p. 13, Bob
Adelman p. 19, Marcos Brindicci/Reuters p. 26, Kapoor Baldev/Sygma p. 29; Getty Images:
Time & Life Pictures p. 10, AFP p. 14, AFP p. 17, Time & Life Pictures p. 18, Hulton Archive
p. 24, AFP p27; iStockphoto: Kriss Russell p. 11; Rex Features: Markus Zeffler p. 2, Markus
Zeffler p. 15, ITV p. 20, ITV p. 21, p. 28; TopFoto: Topham/PA p. 5, Topham Picturepoint
p. 7, The Granger Collection p. 8, Topham/AP p. 16.

Manufactured in China
CPSIA Compliance Information: Batch #WAW1102PK: For Further Information
contact Rosen Publishing, New York, New York at 1-800-237-9932

Contents

On December 1, 1955, in Montgomery, Alabama, an African-American woman named Rosa Parks was ordered to give up her bus seat to a white man. Black people were treated as second-class citizens in the U.S.A. at this time. Rosa refused, and her action sparked off a boycott, a refusal to use the city's buses. The boycott was successful and grew into a campaign for civil rights.

What Is an Activist?

Activists are people who want to influence or change things. They try to persuade other people to support their aims. Each cause they organize is a program of action. Activities might include public speaking, writing, or broadcasting, organizing protests, or even breaking a law that they believe is unjust. Activists may try to persuade elected politicians to bring about change. They may collect the names of people who suport their cause on a petition.

Winning Support

Some activists act on their own. Others may form pressure groups or political parties with other people who share their views. As a cause gains public support, it becomes more effective. Activists may be active locally, nationally, or around the world. Some may wish to bring about change, but others may attempt to prevent change. Some activists, such as those featured in this book, support human rights, peace, or justice. Other activists may support policies that involve violence, racism, or oppression. Each individual must decide whether he or she thinks a cause will make the world a better place or not.

Shaping History

Activists have always shaped history, and this was so in the years between 1900 and 2000. These were times of great change. The population of the world increased rapidly. Huge cities were built, with new factories, roads, and skyscrapers. There were cars on highways, planes in the skies, and spacecraft exploring the solar system. Life-saving medicines were discovered. All kinds of ingenious inventions, from the television to the computer, changed people's lives.

Twentieth-Century Challenges

The twentieth century was also a time of war and mass murder, of poverty, intolerance, and injustice. The natural world was damaged by industry and other human activities. Countless ordinary people tried to tackle such problems. People in Africa and Asia campaigned for the freedom to govern themselves. In many countries, people had to struggle against discrimination due to the color of their skin, their religion, or their political beliefs. Women around the world campaigned for the right to vote.

The Causes Continue...

Some activists of the twentieth century are still remembered today for their achievements. None of them was perfect, but many of them did manage to bring about change through tireless effort and dedication. Just as the problems of the 1900s were rooted in the 1800s, the problems of today are rooted in the last century. By studying the lives of twentieth-century activists, we can all be inspired to take action as citizens of the world.

Protestors try to stop trees from being cut down to make way for a new road at Newbury, Berkshire, UK, in 1995. Many people campaigned to protect the environment at this time.

"People are needed to take up the challenge, strong people, who proclaim the truth, throw it in people's faces, and do what they can with their own two hands." *Abbé Pierre*

5

Mohandas K. Gandhi
Pioneer of Nonviolence

"You must be the change you want to see in the world."

Mohandas K Gandhi

Mohandas Karamchand Gandhi was born in the west of India, in a small state ruled by a prince. His father, Karamchand, was the prince's chief adviser. The prince no longer had any real power, for all of India at that time was governed by Great Britain. Gandhi was very fond of his mother, Putlibai. She was a strong believer in the Hindu faith, who liked to live simply.

England and South Africa
According to local custom, Gandhi married when he was only 13. When he left school, Gandhi persuaded his family to let him go to London, UK, to study law. He passed his exams and found work as a lawyer in South Africa. At that time, this was also part of the British Empire. Gandhi witnessed racial prejudice in South Africa. He campaigned for the voting and taxation rights of Indian workers living there. He organized petitions and founded a political party. Gandhi was jailed by the authorities, but eventually, he succeeded in many of his aims.

Back to India
In 1915, Gandhi returned to India. He saw great poverty, but was impressed by the lives of villagers in the countryside. In the years that followed, he

Name Mohandas Karamchand Gandhi (also known as Mahatma or "great soul")

Born October 2, 1869, in Porbandar, Gujarat, India

Early Life Attended grade school from age seven, then moved to Alfred High School age 12. Studied law in London, UK (1888–91).

Causes Civil rights in South Africa (1893–1914); Indian independence (1916–45); Peace in India (1945–48)

Key Moment The Salt March (1930)

Personal Life Gandhi was a vegetarian. Even when visiting cold countries, he wore only an Indian loin cloth, with a cloak and sandals. Every day he used a simple spinning wheel, which he saw as a symbol of the self-reliance of poor Indian villagers. Gandhi was married to his wife, Kasturbai ("Ba"), from 1882 until her death in 1944.

Died January 30, 1948

Honors October 2, Gandhi's birthday, is a public holiday in India and the UN has declared it the "International Day of Nonviolence."

lived an ever more simple life. He campaigned for poor workers and farmers, and for people from the lowest caste, or class, of Indian society. He called for peace between Hindus and Muslims.

Nonviolent Protest

From 1921, Gandhi led the Indian National Congress to campaign against British rule. As a result, he was jailed from 1922 to 1924. Gandhi used a new method of action known as *satyagraha* or "strength in truth." He called for people to refuse to obey the law. This is known as civil disobedience. At the same time, Gandhi insisted that protest should never be violent.

Freedom and Death

Gandhi became very popular in India. He also won many friends among ordinary people in the UK, when he came to a conference in London in 1931. Gandhi was jailed many more times and often protested by fasting—refusing to eat any food.

After World War II (1939–45), the British government at last agreed to independence for India. However, there was bitter disagreement between Hindus and Muslims, and in the end, two separate states were created—India and Pakistan. Amid terrible violence, Gandhi called for peace.

In 1948, the Mahatma (or "great soul") was assassinated, shot by a Hindu extremist. Gandhi was killed, but his ideas lived on, and are still admired by many people today.

In 1930, Gandhi led a 250-mile (400-km) march from Ahmedabad to Dandi, on the coast. The British controlled the making of salt in India by law. When Gandhi arrived at the sea, he picked up salt that had been deposited naturally on the shore. This action was a symbolic challenge to the UK's rule.

Twentieth-Century Legacy

India's independence from British rule in 1947 marked the start of a new age, in which rule by European powers came to an end in most of Asia and Africa. Gandhi's ideas of civil disobedience and nonviolence still influence activists around the world today. However, Gandhi's ideas failed to prevent political violence in India after independence.

Helen Keller
Activist for the Disabled

"Although the world is full of suffering, it is also full of the overcoming of it."

Helen Keller

Can you imagine a world of darkness, in which you can see nothing and hear nothing? Helen Keller was made blind and deaf by an illness she suffered at the age of just 19 months. Today there are many ways in which deaf and blind people can be helped, but in the 1880s, it was more difficult. Little Helen grew up in a confused and frustrated state, and often had temper tantrums.

Helen's Great Challenge

Her parents, Arthur and Kate, became worried. They sent her to see a specialist, who put them in touch with Alexander Graham Bell. As well as being the inventor of the telephone, he was a researcher into deafness and speech. Helen was soon set up with a young teacher named Anne Sullivan, who was herself partially sighted.

Anne worked wonders with Helen. She taught her how to spell out words with her fingers. Helen was a quick learner and went on to master reading with raised letters, and using Braille, the system of reading for blind people. Speaking without hearing is very hard. Helen had to go to classes to learn how to speak in a way that other people could understand. That took her many years.

Name Helen Adams Keller

Born June 27, 1880, in Tuscumbia, Alabama

Early Life Became deaf and blind at the age of 19 months. Attended the Perkins Institute for the Blind, Boston, Massachusetts; Cambridge School for Young Ladies (1896); Radcliffe College (1900–04)

Causes Fundraising for the blind, international campaigns for the care and education of people with disabilities; supporter of votes for women, peace, civil liberties, and socialism (1904–61)

Key Moment Founding the Helen Keller International organization (1915)

Personal Life Helen Keller's close companions were Anne Sullivan and Polly Thompson. She knew Alexander Graham Bell (inventor of the telephone), the writer Mark Twain, and the movie star Charlie Chaplin. She loved dogs.

Died June 1, 1968

Honors Presidential Medal of Freedom (1964)

In 1900, Helen Keller began to study at Radcliffe, a women's college linked with Harvard University. Anne Sullivan helped her with taking notes. Helen did very well and when she graduated in 1904, she became the first deaf and blind person to do so.

Caring for All

Helen Keller's keen intelligence now tried to make sense of society as a whole. She was interested in ways in which poverty and working in factories might be linked to blindness and deafness, through disease or injury. She became a radical socialist. She soon found that some newspapers who had praised her success in overcoming her disabilities, now abused her for her political views. She supported women's rights, and family planning, too—limiting the number of children had by parents.

International Causes

Helen Keller International was founded in 1915 and today this organization still funds the fight against blindness and disease in the United States, Africa, and Asia. Helen Keller spent most of her life traveling. She persuaded governments to set up schemes for the treatment and education of disabled people, and met with presidents and kings. Wherever she went, she raised money for the blind. She wrote best-selling books and featured in stage shows and movies. She succeeded in changing public attitudes toward disability. Having overcome so many difficulties herself, she spoke with authority and was heard with respect. Helen Keller became ill in 1961 and retired from public life. She died in 1968.

Helen Keller at her 1904 graduation from Radcliffe College. Her fingers are resting on sheets of Braille, the system of raised dots used to represent letters and words, which blind people read by touch.

Twentieth-Century Legacy

Helen Keller made the world view people with disabilities in a different way, and enabled many blind people to receive an education and play an active part in society. She used books, movies, and lecture tours to get her message across. Helen also campaigned on many other social issues, such as women's right to vote and safety in the workplace.

Rachel Carson

Environmentalist

"… the early mornings are strangely silent. where once they were filled with the beauty of birdsong."

Rachel Carson

Rachel Carson had twin passions when she was a child: she loved reading and writing, and she loved studying nature. She was born on a farm in Springdale, Pennsylvania, in 1907. She would spend hours wandering through the fields and observing animals. When she grew up and went to college, it was no surprise that she chose to study English, or that she later changed course to study biology. She became a talented scientist.

Inspiring a Love of Nature

In the 1930s, Rachel needed more income to support her widowed mother, and so she began to write radio scripts and magazine articles about nature and conservation. She edited scientific works, but also, she had the knack of inspiring popular interest in the natural world. She worked for the U.S. government's Fish and Wildlife Service. In 1952, she decided to become a full-time writer. Her books about life in the oceans inspired many readers.

The Poisoned Planet

In the 1950s, the United States became the center of a new approach to farming. Huge amounts of chemicals such as DDT were sprayed on fields to kill pests. This worried Rachel. As a scientist, she

Name Rachel Louise Carson

Born May 27, 1907, in Springdale, Pennsylvania

Early Life Attended local schools in Springdale and Parnassus, then Pennsylvania College for Women (Chatham University), graduating in 1928. She gained a master's degree at Johns Hopkins University in 1932.

Causes Getting people interested in the world of nature (1935–57); protesting against pollution of the environment (1957–64)

Key Moment Publication of her book, *Silent Spring*, in 1962

Personal Life Rachel and her mother moved to Maine in 1953. Rachel's neighbor on Southport Island, Dorothy Freeman, became her closest friend. When Rachel's niece died in 1957, she adopted her five-year-old son, Roger.

Died April 14, 1964

Honors Presidential Medal of Freedom (1980)

knew that the environment was made up of complicated networks of life forms, and these depended on each other for survival.

Rachel could see that the chemicals also killed insects that were not pests. Birds and other creatures that ate poisoned seeds or insects also died. The survival of whole species was threatened. Rain washed pesticides into streams, rivers, and oceans. Crops eaten by humans were also now full of dangerous chemicals.

A small plane flies low over farmland, spraying the crops with pesticides. It was the effect of pesticides such as these on the environment and on the food chain that so concerned Rachel Carson.

For a Greener Future

Rachel Carson conducted four years of scientific research on the effects of pesticides on the environment. She campaigned for harmful chemicals to be replaced. She had the support of many naturalists and scientists, but she infuriated the big chemical companies—especially when she wrote of her fears in a book published in 1962, called *Silent Spring*.

Public opinion soon came to share her point of view. Rachel Carson was called to give scientific evidence to U.S. government committees. Sadly, weakened by cancer, she died in 1964.

Twentieth-Century Legacy

It could be said that Rachel Carson started the modern environmental movement. Having studied nature all her life, she was one of the first people to realize the danger to the environment from using dangerous chemicals in farming. In the 1980s and 1990s, her ideas were taken up by the environmental movement around the world.

Abbé Pierre
Helper of the Poor and Homeless

"People are needed to take up the challenge, strong people, who proclaim the truth, throw it in people's faces, and do what they can with their own two hands."

Abbé Pierre

Name Henri-Antoine Grouès, known as Abbé Pierre ("Peter the priest")

Born August 5, 1912, in Lyon, France

Early Life Henri-Antoine was one of eight children born to a wealthy Catholic family. He was an avid boy scout and helped his father with charity work for the poor. At the age of 16, he decided he wanted to become a monk, an ambition he fulfilled in 1931. He joined the French Resistance movement during World War II (1939–45), using the code name "Abbé Pierre."

Causes French resistance to the Nazis (1939–44); Emmaus communities for the homeless (from 1949); Campaigns for better housing, international human rights, refugees, and asylum seekers (1945–2007)

Key Moment The Uprising of Kindness (1954)

Personal Life Abbé Pierre was a familiar figure in France, with his beret, black cloak, and beard. He often annoyed politicians and senior figures in the Catholic Church, but was hugely popular with the general public.

Died January 22, 2007

Honors Grand Cross of the Légion d'Honneur (Legion of Honor, 2004)

Henri-Antoine Grouès was born in Lyon, France, in 1912. He came from a prosperous family, but spent his whole life campaigning for the poor and the homeless. In 1931, he gave up all his possessions and became a monk, taking the name Brother Philip. He later ran an orphanage.

Grouès' experiences during World War II (1939–45) made him tough and resourceful. He joined French fighters who were resisting the German occupation of their country. They gave him the code name "Abbé Pierre." At this time, Germany was governed by violent racists called Nazis, and the Abbé helped Jews and political opponents of the Nazis escape to Switzerland.

Emmaus Communities

After the war, Abbé Pierre campaigned against nuclear weapons, which had been used at the end of the war in 1945. For a time, he tried to change society though party politics, but in 1949, he decided instead to try a social experiment. He founded a community for the poor and homeless, near Paris. He named it "Emmaus," after a village described in the Bible. He even gained a large amount of funding by winning a game show on the radio.

Following deaths during the bitterly cold winter of 1954, Abbé Pierre used the press to call for aid for the homeless and hungry. The response was an astonishing "uprising of kindness." Vast amounts of money and offers of practical help flooded in. Soon, Emmaus communities were being founded around the world.

In the Right or the Wrong

Abbé Pierre never gave up. He supported refugees, people fleeing from war or oppression. He gave his support to squatters, people illegally occupying empty property. He criticized the world money system, which seemed to make poor countries even poorer. He traveled the world, fearlessly attacking racism and injustice.

In his old age, he sometimes angered his supporters. In 1996, he expressed support for a friend who had written a book questioning facts about the persecution of Jews by the Nazis. The Abbé immediately made it clear that he did not agree with the content of the book himself—but he had already caused great offense.

However, in the end, nobody could really question the Abbé's own record. Had he not risked his own life helping Jews during the war—as well as countless other people suffering from hardship and persecution over the years? By the time of his death, at the age of 94, this tireless, passionate, activist had made a real difference.

This photograph was taken in August 1955. It shows Abbé Pierre visiting a group of homeless people in Paris, on the bank of the Seine River. The people were sleeping in tents provided by the Emmaus organization, which was founded by Abbé Pierre.

Twentieth-Century Legacy

Abbé Pierre's politics caused argument and discussion, but he campaigned tirelessly and effectively for the poor and the homeless, and for refugees around the world. The charity is still very active today.

13

Nelson Mandela
The Man Who Defeated Apartheid

> "It always seems impossible until it is done."
>
> *Nelson Mandela*

Apartheid means keeping people of different color separate. The word was used to describe the racist system of government in South Africa from 1948 until 1990, when the civil rights of citizens depended on the color of their skin. Black people were not allowed to vote. They were forced to live in certain areas and do certain jobs. They could not marry white people, or even sit on the same bench as them in a park.

The "Troublemaker"

Mandela, one of the many who fought against apartheid, and defeated it, was born in 1918. He belonged to a family that had once been rulers in the Transkei region. However, at the time of Mandela's birth, South Africa was a part of the British Empire. The boy's African first name, Rolihlahla, means "troublemaker," and from an early age he spoke out against injustice. He was forced to leave Fort Hare University after taking part in student protests.

Lawyer on Trial

Mandela went on to study law. He later became a lawyer and defended poor black people in court. Mandela was soon playing a leading role in the African National Congress (ANC), a political

Name Nelson Rolihlahla Mandela

Born July 18, 1918, in Mvezo, Transkei, South Africa

Early Life Attended mission school, Clarkebury Boarding Institute (age 16), Healdtown College (1937), Fort Hare University (1937), and studied law at Witwatersrand University (1939)

Causes Challenging racism in South Africa (1939–47); opposing the system of apartheid brought in by the South African government (1948–94); building a democratic South Africa (1990–99)

Key Moment The Rivonia Trial (1963–64)

Personal Life The name "Nelson" was given to Rolihlahla by one of his teachers. Mandela married three times and had six children.

Honors Nobel Peace Prize, jointly with South African president F. W. de Klerk (1993)

movement that was opposed to apartheid. He led many protest campaigns. He and other ANC members were arrested in 1956 and charged with treason. The trial dragged on for five years, but at the end of this time, the activists walked free.

Which Way Forward?

In 1960, South African police shot dead peaceful protestors during a demonstration at Sharpeville. The ANC was banned. Mandela had always admired the nonviolence of Gandhi, but he now decided that the South African government had closed down all peaceful methods of bringing about change. More violent protests, even an armed uprising, might be necessary.

Years in Prison

In 1962, Mandela was arrested once more and imprisoned. New charges were brought against him, along with other ANC leaders arrested near Rivonia. In a moving speech at the "Rivonia Trial," Mandela explained how he was prepared to die for freedom. In 1964, he was given a life sentence. For 18 years, he was imprisoned offshore on Robben Island, and forced to break stones in a quarry. In 1984, he was moved to a prison in Cape Town, and four years later to Paarl. He was finally released in 1990 after 27 years.

Elected President

The apartheid system now crumbled. Democratic elections for all South Africans were held in 1994. Nelson Mandela was elected South Africa's first black president. He came to be much admired throughout South Africa and all over the world, even by his former enemies.

Nelson Mandela with supporters, voting in the 1994 elections in South Africa.

Twentieth-Century Legacy

Nelson Mandela showed that even when he was locked up in jail, he could inspire others by his example. He showed not only how to resist injustice, but also how to build peace and trust. In the 1960s, many white people called him a terrorist. By the 1990s, he was respected around the world as an outstanding leader.

Peter Benenson

Founder of Amnesty International

> "When I first lit the Amnesty candle, I had in mind the old Chinese proverb: 'Better light a candle than curse the darkness.'"
>
> *Peter Benenson*

Amnesty International is an organization that campaigns on behalf of "prisoners of conscience"—people who are imprisoned for their ideas or beliefs. The word *amnesty* means "pardon." Members of Amnesty write to prisoners to show their support. They write to governments to protest about injustice, lack of human rights, torture, unfair trials, executions, and murders. Amnesty International is respected—but also feared—by governments around the world, for it is impartial but relentless in its investigations.

Victims of Dictatorship

Amnesty was founded by Peter Benenson, who was born in 1921. His father, Harold Solomon, had been a British army officer. His mother, Flora Benenson, was the daughter of a Russian banker. Both of Peter's parents were from Jewish families. In 1937, at only 16, young Peter organized help for victims of the Spanish Civil War, when General Franco overthrew the elected government of Spain. Peter went on to help raise money for Jews fleeing persecution in Nazi Germany. During World War II (1939–45), he left his studies and worked at a secret center at Bletchley Park, in the UK, where his job was breaking German codes.

Name Peter James Henry Benenson (born Solomon)

Born July 31, 1921, in London, UK

Early Life The poet W. H. Auden was Peter's private tutor. Peter went on to be a pupil at Eton College.

Causes Relief for victims of the Spanish Civil War and Nazi Germany (1937–39); legal work for international human rights (1950s); Amnesty International (from 1961)

Key Moment Reading about a political trial in Portugal, in 1960

Personal Life Peter's father died in 1930. In 1939, Peter adopted his mother's family name in honor of his grandfather. During World War II, he met his first wife, Margaret Anderson. The marriage ended in 1972. In 1973, Peter married his second wife, Susan Booth.

Died February 25, 2005

Honors Peter Benenson refused to accept most personal honors. Amnesty International was awarded the Nobel Peace Prize in 1977.

For Human Rights

After the war, Peter became a lawyer who specialized in human rights. He attended trials in Spain and Cyprus. In 1957, he was one of a group of lawyers who founded JUSTICE, a human rights pressure group based in the United Kingdom. He persuaded the UK government to send international observers to the trial of Nelson Mandela and others in South Africa.

Challenging Injustice

One day in 1960, Peter Benenson was traveling to work on a London Underground train, reading the newspaper. A report from Portugal, which at that time was ruled by a dictator, made him very angry. Two Portuguese students had been sentenced to seven years in prison, for raising their glasses and drinking a toast "To Liberty." When even law courts dispensed injustice, what, Peter asked, could be done to change things? The answer, he decided, was to get ordinary people around the world to protest.

A Candle in the Darkness

The "Appeal for Amnesty" was begun in 1961, with the help of lawyers, publishers, and writers. The organization grew very quickly and soon became a powerful force. Peter later retired because of ill health, and he also had some disagreements with other leading members. However, he never stopped working for the oppressed and for prisoners of conscience. Today, Amnesty International has more than 2.2 million members in more than 150 countries and regions around the world.

The symbol of Amnesty International is a candle surrounded by barbed wire. It is displayed at press conferences, vigils, and demonstrations.

Twentieth-Century Legacy

Peter Benenson's aim was not just to be an activist himself, but to make everybody an activist, around the world. Amnesty became a great international organization with the power to influence governments. Its success may be measured in the growth of international law and in the release of countless prisoners of conscience around the world.

17

Martin Luther King

Civil Rights Activist

"I have a dream that one day this nation will rise up and live out the true meaning of its creed: 'We hold these truths to be self-evident: that all men are created equal.'"

Martin Luther King, Jr.

Name Martin Luther King, Jr. (born Michael King, Jr.)

Born January 15, 1929, in Atlanta, Georgia

Early Life He sang in his church choir as a boy and attended Booker T. Washington High School. He then went to Morehouse College (age 15), and the Crozer Theological Seminary in Pennsylvania, leaving to become a Baptist Minister in 1948.

Causes Montgomery Improvement Association (1955); full-time civil rights activist (1959–68); opposition to the Vietnam War (1965–68); Poor People's campaign (1968)

Key Moment Speech to marchers in Washington, DC: "I have a dream…"

Personal Life Renamed Martin Luther in honor of the German Protestant reformer (1483–1546). He married Coretta Scott in 1953.

Died April 4, 1968

Honors Nobel Peace Prize (1964). Martin Luther King, Jr. Day is held each year in the United States, on the third Monday in January.

Martin Luther King, Jr. was born in 1929, to an African-American family. Although slavery had been abolished in the United States since 1865, racist laws in the south had ensured that African Americans remained second-class citizens. Even in King's own day, black people were generally prevented from voting. They could not go to the same schools as whites, or sit in the same restaurants. Sometimes black people were murdered, or "lynched," by angry mobs.

Boycotts and Buses

Martin Luther King was determined to fight the injustice of racial segregation and to campaign for the rights of his people—and all people. His first great victory was the Montgomery Bus Boycott of 1955–56. This was organized when a black woman named Rosa Parks (see page 4) refused to give up her seat on a bus to a white man. King and other activists persuaded people not to use the city's buses in protest. At last, segregation on the buses was made illegal.

Civil Disobedience

In 1957, King founded the Southern Christian Leadership Conference. This organization worked alongside student associations and other groups such as the Congress of Racial Equality (CORE) to change unjust laws. Protestors sat down at whites-only lunch counters and refused to be moved. They challenged segregation in schools and colleges. They were often attacked by angry opponents and beaten by police. King was arrested several times. He was an admirer of Gandhi's ideas, believing that civil disobedience should be nonviolent. A growing number of African Americans disagreed with this, believing that more extreme action was needed.

"I have a dream..."

Martin Luther King was a great public speaker, in the tradition of African-American speakers. He made his most moving speech in 1963, in front of 250,000 protestors in Washington, DC. "I have a dream…" he repeated, as he spoke of his vision for the future.

In 1965, a new Voting Rights Act was at last passed, enforcing black people's right to vote. In 1966, King began a campaign against war and poverty. His life ended tragically in 1968, when he was murdered by a gunman in Memphis, Tennessee. The news was received with grief and violence. There were riots in cities across the United States.

Martin Luther King makes his "I have a dream" speech in 1963, in Washington, DC.

Twentieth-Century Legacy

Martin Luther King played a key role in bringing segregation to an end in the United States. He inspired not only African Americans, but people of all backgrounds, and not just Americans but people in many parts of the world. Today, some of King's dreams have come true. The United States has an African-American president. However, if he were alive today, King would still be greatly concerned about poverty and violence.

Chico Mendes
Protector of the Rain Forest

"At first, I thought I was fighting to save rubber trees, then I thought I was fighting to save the Amazon rain forest. Now I realize I am fighting for humanity."

Chico Mendes

Name Francisco Alves Mendes Filho, known as Chico Mendes

Born December 15, 1944, in Porto Rico, Acre, Brazil

Early Life Chico came from a poor Brazilian family who made a living by tapping rubber trees in the Amazon rain forest. He started work at the age of nine. He could not read or write until he was 14.

Causes Improving the conditions of rubber workers (from 1964); protecting the rain forest (1970s); campaigning against road building (1986–87)

Key Moment Mendes organizes the first *empate* or "stand-off," in which workers were persuaded not to cut down the forest (1976).

Personal Life Chico Mendes married his first wife, Maria Eunice Feitosa, in 1969. He was later divorced and married a second wife, Ilzamar.

Died December 22, 1988

Honors Mendes's life has inspired many plays, movies, and songs. A species of South American river fish was named in his honor. He won the United Nations Global 500 Award for Environmental Achievement in 1987.

In the first half of the twentieth century, fortunes were made from the rubber trees that grew naturally in the Amazon rain forest. Many poor people went to remote areas of Brazil, to seek work as "tappers." They placed cups to collect the sap, which oozed from cuts in the trunk. This "latex" was processed to make rubber.

Hard Times

Chico Mendes's father, Francisco, was one of these workers. He was lame and desperately poor. Chico, who was born in 1944, received no schooling and went to work as a tapper at the age of nine. By this time, the rubber industry was in rapid decline.

The Union Man

In 1962, Chico made friends with a political activist named Euclides Fernandez Tavora. He taught Chico to read and write and some of Tavora's ideas rubbed off on the young man. In the 1970s, Chico founded a trade union called the Xapuri Rural Workers' Union. In 1985, he set up the National Council of Rubber Tappers.

Forest in Flames

The 1970s and 1980s saw the Amazon rain forest threatened for the first time in history. The Brazilian government decided to open up the forest for development. Miners, ranchers, and loggers moved in. Vast areas of forest were cleared by burning, poisoning the Earth's atmosphere. The indigenous people who lived in the forest were attacked by the incomers. The land rights of the poor rubber tappers were ignored.

Stop the Loggers!

Mendes wanted to create reserves where rubber tappers could still operate, and at the same time protect the natural environment. In 1976, he organized the first *empate* or "standoff." This became a common method of protest. A hundred or more men and women would enter a logging camp. They would try to dissuade or prevent the workmen from destroying trees. Chico met with some success. He also made many enemies among the ruthless ranchers and developers.

Death of an Activist

In 1985–86, Mendes campaigned against a new road that was to be built through the forest with international financial support. He flew to Miami, Florida, and managed to get the project postponed and changed. On December 22, 1988, Chico—like many other protestors before him—was shot dead by ranchers. However, by then the outside world knew about the crisis in the Amazon rain forest, thanks to his lifetime of protesting.

Behind Chico Mendes, the rain forest is destroyed. The forest is one of the planet's most important natural resources.

Twentieth-Century Legacy

Chico Mendes's life and death helped to alert the world to the dangers of destroying one of the planet's most important resources, the Amazon rain forest. He also highlighted human suffering and injustice.

21

Aung San Suu Kyi

Activist for Democracy

"… even under the most crushing state machinery, courage rises up again and again, for fear is not the natural state of civilized man."

Aung San Suu Kyi

Aung San Suu Kyi was born in Rangoon, Burma, in 1945. Her father was a respected and popular figure, who negotiated freedom for his country from British rule. Sadly, he was murdered before independence came in 1947. When her mother became Burmese ambassador to India in 1960, Aung San Suu Kyi took up her studies there. She later went to Oxford University, in the UK, and also spent a year in the United States, working for the United Nations. In 1972, she married a British scholar, Dr. Michael Aris.

Speaking for the People

In 1988, Aung San Suu Kyi returned to Burma, because her mother was very ill. She arrived at a stormy time in Burmese politics. After 22 years of repressive military rule, thousands of people took to the streets demanding democracy. Many protestors were killed by soldiers. Aung San Suu Kyi called for free elections and spoke to a vast crowd outside a historic temple, the Shwedagon Pagoda. That September military rule was brought back under the State Law and Order Restoration Council (SLORC). Aung San Suu Kyi responded by

Name Aung San Suu Kyi

Born June 19, 1945, in Rangoon, Burma (now called Yangon, Myanmar)

Early Life Educated at schools in Burma, then at Lady Shri Ram College, India (graduated 1964), St. Hugh's College, Oxford University, UK (1969), and School of African and Oriental Studies, London University, UK (1985)

Causes Democracy and human rights in Burma (from 1988)

Key Moment Founding the National League for Democracy in 1988

Personal Life Married to Dr. Michael Aris in 1972, she has two sons. Her husband died in 1999.

Honors Nobel Peace Prize (1991)

helping to found a National League for Democracy (NLD). She was inspired by the ideas of Gandhi and by her Buddhist faith.

Banned!

Although SLORC banned public meetings, Aung San Suu Kyi traveled around the country to speak. She was in great danger. Many of her supporters were arrested, beaten, or killed.

In 1989, she was placed under house arrest and banned from leaving her home. Even so, when a general election was held in 1990, the NLD won a sweeping victory. However, Aung San Suu Kyi did not head a new government. SLORC refused to hand over power.

House Arrest

Since then, Aung San Suu Kyi has been repeatedly detained in her home. She has always known that if she leaves Burma, the government will not allow her back into the country. When her husband Michael became sick with cancer, the Burmese government would not even let him visit her from the UK. He died in 1999. In May 2009, Aung San Suu Kyi was put on trial, accused of breaking the conditions of her detention. Her supporters claimed that this was to prevent her standing at the 2010 general election. The treatment of Aung San Suu Kyi has drawn world attention to the Burmese government's oppressive dictatorship.

Supporters of Burmese democracy hold up posters of Aung San Suu Kyi during a march in London.

Twentieth-Century Legacy

Under Burma's dictatorship, Aung San Suu Kyi has been unable to campaign in public because of her detention. However, her long detention has in itself become a symbol of resistance to dictatorship and oppression.

23

Emmeline Pankhurst is hauled away from a protest outside Buckingham Palace, London, in 1914.

Name Emmeline Pankhurst

Born July 15, 1858, in Manchester, UK

Early Life Emmeline loved to read as a little girl. She was brought up to have a keen interest in women's rights. She went to school in Manchester and when she was 15, to a school in Paris, France.

Causes Votes for women (1872–1918)

Key Moment Founding the Women's Social and Political Union in 1903

Personal Life Emmeline married a lawyer, Richard Pankhust, in 1879. He died in 1898. They had five children. Their three daughters, Christabel, Sylvia, and Adela all became suffragettes, but later disagreements over policy divided the family. After 1918, Emmeline supported the British Empire, opposed communism, and joined the Conservative Party.

Died June 14, 1928

Honors A statue was erected in Victoria Tower Gardens, London (1930).

Emmeline Pankhurst
Suffragette

In the early 1900s, few countries allowed all their citizens to vote in elections. Since the 1800s, women and some men had campaigned for women's suffrage (the right to vote). They were called suffragists.

An activist named Emmeline Pankhurst decided that women in the UK would not succeed unless they took more extreme action. She and her supporters became known as "suffragettes."

Protest and Prison

In 1903, Emmeline Pankhurst and her daughters founded the Women's Social and Political Union (WSPU). The members of the WSPU began by holding meetings and collecting signatures on petitions. Later they became more extreme. They smashed windows, chained themselves to railings, and set fire to buildings. An activist named Emily Davison was killed by a horse when she ran on the track as a protest at the Epsom races. Many suffragettes were sent to prison, where some of them went on hunger strike, refusing to eat.

Winning the Vote

During World War I (1914–18), the WSPU stopped its actions and supported the war effort. With so many soldiers away fighting, women began to take on work that only men had done before the war, and won a new respect. British women over the age of 30 were finally given the vote in 1918, and women over 21, in 1929, shortly after the death of Emmeline Pankhurst.

Bertrand Russell

Peace Activist

Bertrand Russell came from a family that had played an important part in the UK government for centuries. Despite this, Russell rejected old-fashioned ideas. He was a philosopher, historian, and mathematician who spoke out about the world around him.

World Wars

Russell opposed World War I (1914–18), and supported those who refused to fight. His protesting cost him his job at Cambridge University. In 1918, he was sent to prison, because he wrote an article calling for peace. He did not oppose World War II (1939–45), because he believed that the Nazis could only be defeated by force. In 1945, this war was ended when U.S. aircraft dropped nuclear bombs on two cities in Japan, causing utter devastation to the country.

Peace and Justice

In the 1950s, Bertrand Russell met with leading thinkers, such as Albert Einstein, to discuss his fears for the future. He became president of the Campaign for Nuclear Disarmament (CND) in 1957, and in 1960 set up a radical peace group called the Committee of 100. Russell, at 88, was imprisoned when he called for civil disobedience. In 1963, he set up the Bertrand Russell Peace Foundation, which still works for peace and justice today. Russell worked for this cause to the end of his life and died in 1970.

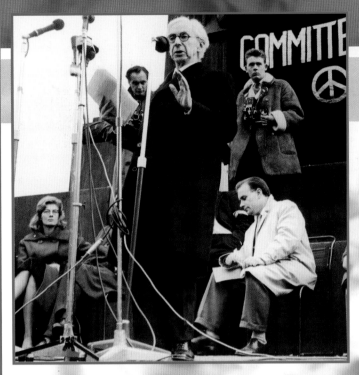

Bertrand Russell calls for an end to nuclear weapons.

Name Bertrand Arthur William Russell, 3rd Earl Russell

Born May 18, 1872, in Trellech, Monmouthshire, Wales

Early Life Russell's mother, father, and sister all died when he was very young. He and his brother were raised by his grandmother. He studied at Cambridge University, in the UK.

Causes Men's League for Women's Suffrage (1907); Against World War I (1914–18); for Educational reform (1927–32); for world government (1930s–60s); against nuclear weapons (1957–70); against the Vietnam War (1966–70)

Key Moment Establishing the Bertrand Russell Peace Foundation (1963)

Personal Life Bertrand Russell held views about morality, society, and marriage that were unusual for his generation. He married four times and had three children.

Died February 2, 1970

Honors He was awarded the Nobel Prize for Literature in 1950 for his writings about "humanitarian ideals and freedom of thought."

Mothers protest against the disappearance of 30,000 people in Argentina, including that of Azucenza Villaflor. Her photograph is on the right of the poster on the wall above the activists in this picture.

Name Azucena Villaflor

Born April 7, 1924, in Avellaneda, Buenos Aires, Argentina

Early Life Azucena was the daughter of Emma Nits and Florentino Villaflor, a worker in a wool factory. From the age of 16 she worked as a secretarial assistant in an electrical goods company.

Cause Mothers of the Plaze de Mayo (1977)

Key Moment The disappearance of her son Néstor and her daughter-in-law Raquel

Personal Life Azucena married Pedro De Vicenti, a trade unionist, in 1949. She had four children.

Died Date unknown, but probably December 1977

Honors May Pyramid memorial, Plaza del Mayo, Buenos Aires (2005), which is still a rallying point for the Mothers and their supporters.

Azucena Villaflor
Mother of the "Disappeared"

Many causes are started by idealists or activists. Azucena Villaflor was just a woman leading a regular life, caring for her family, when she became caught up in terrible events.

The Dirty War

In March 1976, military leaders seized power in Argentina. Their new government began a state of terror, which became known as the "Dirty War." Trade unionists, socialists, communists, and democrats were kidnapped or imprisoned and tortured. Many were murdered.

"Dónde están?"—Where Are They?

In November 1976, Azucena's son Néstor disappeared, along with his wife, Raquel Mangin. Azucena went to the government offices to make inquiries. Month after month, she was sent away without any news. She soon met other mothers searching for relatives who had disappeared. On April 30, 1977, she and 13 other mothers decided to protest on the Plaza del Mayo, the main square in Buenos Aires. Every week they returned.

In desperation, on December 10, 1977, the "Mothers of the Plaza" placed an appeal in the newspaper, listing the names of their disappeared children. That same night, Azucena was seized from her home and taken to a camp. She was never seen alive again. Long after military rule had ended, her remains were discovered and identified.

Wangari Maathai

The "Tree Woman"

Raised in a Kenyan village in the 1940s, Wangari used to fetch water from the river for her mother. The countryside was green and clean. After working hard at school, Wangari won a scholarship to study in the U.S.A. When she returned to her country years later, the river had dried up and the land was dry and dusty.

The Green Belt Movement

In 1976, Wangari Maathai founded the Green Belt Movement. Her idea was for women from the villages to plant trees, to stop Kenya's landscape from turning into desert. Tree roots trap moisture and stop the soil blowing away. This plan not only improved the environment, but gave women the feeling that they had the power to change things. Wangari became known as "the tree woman." Thanks to her, over 40 million trees have been planted in the Kenyan countryside.

Working for Progress

Wangari soon made powerful political enemies. When she opposed building development in Nairobi's Uhuru Park, she and her supporters were beaten by police. Wangari began to campaign on a range of issues, including social justice, civil rights, and tackling corruption.

Wangari was elected to parliament in 2002 and has worked with the United Nations in areas such as education and the environment.

Wangari Maathai with the future U.S. president, Barack Obama, in 2006.

Name Wangari Muta Maathai

Born April 1, 1940, in Ihithe, Nyeri, Kenya

Early Life Wangari Maatahi was born to a Kikuyu farming family, the eldest of six children. She attended Ihithe Primary School, and Loreto Convent School, Limuru, and won a scholarship to Mount St. Scholastica College, in the U.S.A. (1964). She was awarded a master's degree at the University of Pittsburgh (1966) and a PhD from the University of Nairobi in Kenya (1971).

Causes Kenyan environmental campaign (from 1976); women's rights and civil rights in Kenya (1980s–90s)

Key Moment Founding the Green Belt Movement (1977)

Personal Life In 1969, she married a politician named Mwangi Mathai. They later divorced. She has three children, Waweru, Wanjira, and Muta.

Honors Nobel Peace Prize (2004)

Bob Geldof visited Ethiopia during the mid-1980s as part of his campaign to raise money to help the people affected by famine and drought in the country.

Name Robert ("Bob") Frederick Zenon Geldof

Born October 5, 1951, in Dun Laoghaire, Ireland

Early Life Attended Blackrock College, near Dublin. Took odd jobs after leaving school, and then worked as a music journalist for a Canadian weekly newspaper. In 1975, he became the lead singer of a band named the Boomtown Rats, which had big hits in 1978–79.

Causes Band Aid (1984); Live Aid (1985); founding the Commission for Africa (2004); Live 8 (2005)

Key Moment Seeing images of famine in Ethiopia (1985)

Personal Life Longtime association and marriage with music journalist Paula Yates. The couple divorced in 1996. Yates died four years later. Four children (one adopted).

Honors Honorary knighthood, UK (1986)

Bob Geldof
Organizer of "Live Aid"

Some activists become famous because of the causes they support. Some famous people take up causes because they realize that they can use their celebrity to win support.

"Feed the world..."

In 1984, rock star Bob Geldof was horrified to see images of children starving in Ethiopia. He decided to do something about it. With the musician Midge Ure, he wrote a song called *Do They Know It's Christmas?* It was recorded by a group of famous singers under the name of Band Aid. Its sales raised $12 million for food aid to Ethiopia. In 1985, Geldof went a step further. He organized a massive concert called Live Aid, which was watched on television by 400 million people worldwide. Geldof swore and shouted as he urged the public to donate money. In the end, Live Aid may have raised up to $225 million for African famine relief.

Action for Africa

Africa's many problems could not be solved by donations of money alone. In 2004 and 2005, Geldof launched new campaigns, trying to tackle wider issues, such as debt, water supply, AIDS, and corruption. He organized more concerts and held meetings with the world's most powerful politicians. Bob Geldof succeeded in getting ordinary people to realize what was happening in Africa, and his concerts showed for the first time how large amounts of money could be raised for emergency aid.

Arundhati Roy

Writer and Activist

Arundhati Roy became famous when she wrote a prize-winning novel called *The God of Small Things*. It was published in 1997. People wondered what her next novel would be about. As it happened, she turned to writing about political, social, and environmental problems instead. And she began to support causes.

Stop the Dams!

Arundhati gave her prize money to the Save Narmada Movement, whose leading activist was a woman named Medha Patkar. This organization opposed plans to build a series of huge dams on the Narmada River, in India. Roy and other activists were worried by the design and function of the dams, by threats to the environment, and by the forced removal of half a million people from their homes and villages.

Making a Difference

Arundhati Roy also took up other causes. She opposed India's testing of nuclear weapons. She supported independence for the troubled territory of Kashmir, claimed by both India and Pakistan. In the 2000s, she campaigned against the policies of the United States and its allies in Iraq, Afghanistan, and Palestine. She has argued more widely for human rights and the upholding of international law, and against global economics. She believes that it takes personal, passionate, and outspoken commitment to make a difference.

Arundhati Roy leading the march against plans to build dams on the Narmada River.

Name Suzanna Arundhati Roy

Born November 24, 1961, in Shillong, Meghalaya, India

Early Life Roy's mother was a women's rights activist. Her father was a tea planter. She was raised in Amaynam, Kerala, and educated at Corpus Christi school, Kottayam, and Lawrence School, Lovedale, Tamil Nadu. Roy studied architecture in New Delhi.

Causes Supporter of the campaign against India's Narmada dam; activist for the environment, human rights, and international law; opponent of nuclear weapons and globalization

Key Moment The essay *The Greater Common Good* (1999)

Personal Life Lives in New Delhi. Married her second husband, filmmaker Pradip Krishen, in 1984.

Honors Booker Prize for *The God of Small Things*, (1997), Sydney Peace Prize (2004)

29

Timeline

1902 Mohandas K. Gandhi continues to campaign against repression in South Africa.

1903 The Pankhursts found the Women's Social and Political Union, campaigning for UK women's right to vote.

1904 Helen Keller, deaf and blind, begins to campaign for the education and care of the disabled in the United States.

1914–18 World War I is opposed by pacifists across Europe, including Bertrand Russell.

1920 Gandhi starts noncooperation campaign against British rule in India.

1930 Gandhi leads the Salt March in India.

1937 German anti-Nazi activist Martin Niemöller is imprisoned.

1938 Start of Aboriginal rights campaigns in Australia.

1939–45 World War II

1942 The Oxford Committee for Famine Relief (later known as Oxfam) is founded in the UK.

1949 Abbé Pierre founds "Emmaus communities" for the homeless in France.

1955 The Montgomery Bus Boycott challenges segregation in the U.S.A.: Rosa Parks and Martin Luther King are at the forefront of the campaign.

1957 Rachel Carson starts to campaign against the use of harmful pesticides in the U.S.A.

1958 Campaign for Nuclear Disarmament (CND) is launched in the UK.

1961 Amnesty International is founded in the UK by Peter Benenson.

1963 Martin Luther King's speech in Washington, DC: "I have a dream..."

1964 The Rivonia trial in South Africa ends with the jailing of Nelson Mandela, leading opponent of apartheid segregation in South Africa.

1966 The charity Shelter is launched in the UK to campaign against poor housing and homelessness.

1969 The Friends of the Earth environmental movement is founded in the United States.

1971 Founders of the Greenpeace environmental movement set sail from Canada to protest against nuclear testing.

1976 Chico Mendes organizes the first *empate* or standoff against developers in the Amazon rain forest.

1976 Wangari Maathai founds the Green Belt Movement in Kenya.

1985 Live Aid concerts are organized by campaigning rock star Bob Geldof to relieve famine in Africa.

1988 Aung San Suu Kyi launches a campaign for democracy in Burma.

1989 Chinese prodemocracy activists are killed in Tiananmen Square, Beijing.

1997 Indian writer Arundhati Roy starts campaigning by joining protestors against the Narmada dam.

Further Reading and Web Sites

After Gandhi: One Hundred Years of Nonviolent Resistance
by Anne Sibley O'Brien and Perry Edmond O'Brien
(Charlesbridge Publishing, 2009)

Martin Luther King, Jr: Civil Rights Leader
by Robert Jakoubek
(Checkmark Books, 2008)

Women's Suffrage In America
by Elizabeth Frost-Knappman and Kathryn Cullen-Dupont
(Facts on File, 2004)

Web Sites

Due to the changing nature of Internet links, PowerKids Press has developed an online list of Web sites related to the subject of this book. This site is updated regularly. Please use this link to access this list:
http://www.powerkidslinks.com/tcl/activ

Glossary

activist a person who works hard for a cause.

apartheid The system of separating people according to the color of their skin, as enforced in South Africa between 1948 and 1990. The word comes from the Afrikaans language.

assassinate To murder someone, especially for political or religious reasons.

boycott A form of protest in which people refuse to buy goods or services, or have other dealings.

cause An organized and ongoing movement that aims to produce a political, social, or commercial outcome.

charity An organization that provides aid or relief to people in need of medical, financial, or other assistance.

civil disobedience Refusing to obey the law or cooperate with government, as a form of protest.

communist Someone who believes in state control of the economy, resources, and assets.

democracy Government by the people or by their elected representatives.

dictatorship A government with absolute power, run by an unelected leadership.

Disappeared, the A term used in Central and South America to describe people who disappear, having been kidnapped, imprisoned, or murdered by police, soldiers, or government agents.

discrimination Favoring one person or thing above another.

economics The way in which a society organizes money, work, and taxation.

environmentalist Someone who cares for the natural world.

globalization Trading (for example) on a worldwide rather than a local or national scale.

house arrest Being detained in one's own house and denied free movement.

human rights The basic needs that are generally believed to be necessary for people to lead a decent life, such as food, health, and education.

independence Freedom for a territory to govern itself as a nation.

indigenous Originating in a country, native born.

international law The legislation that governs relations between different countries.

intolerance Not showing consideration for other people or their opinions.

mass murder The systematic killing of large numbers of people, as in the Holocaust organized by the Nazis in Germany before and during World War II.

military rule Government by military officers instead of elected representatives.

nonviolence Not using violent or intimidating behavior during a campaign or protest.

nuclear weapons Any weapon that relies on nuclear fission or fusion to create a massive explosion. Nuclear bombs destroy vast numbers of people instantly, and kill many more over a long period from radiation.

occupation The seizure and ongoing control of one territory or nation by another.

oppression Using authority or power over other people in a cruel or unjust way.

pacifist Someone who is against the use of violence.

party politics Activities carried out by formally organized political parties.

petition A formal request for action from a government or other body, often signed by many supporters of a particular campaign.

prejudice Making one's mind up, generally unfavorably, without consideration or reason.

pressure group A group of people who come together in order to persuade politicians or others to adopt a particular policy.

radical Going to the root of a problem, fundamental or extreme.

repressive Putting down opposition, preventing free speech.

segregation Keeping people of a different color apart in society.

socialist Someone who believes in state or community ownership of resources.

suffragette An activist for women's right to vote, who was prepared to use illegal or violent methods of protest.

trade union A group of workers who come together in order to campaign for better wages or working conditions.

treason The crime of betraying a ruler or a state.

Index